Intended Place

Wick Poetry First Book Series
Maggie Anderson, Editor

Already the World
Victorial Redel   GERALD STERN, JUDGE

Likely
Lisa Coffman   ALICIA SUSKIN OSTRIKER, JUDGE

Intended Place
Rosemary Willey   YUSEF KOMUNYAKAA, JUDGE

Intended Place

Poems by
Rosemary Willey

The Kent State
University Press
Kent, Ohio, &
London, England

© 1997 by Rosemary Willey
All rights reserved.
Library of Congress Catalog Card Number 97-12240
ISBN 0-87338-581-0 (cloth)
ISBN 0-87338-584-5 (pbk.)
Manufactured in the United States of America

05 04 03 02 01 00 99 98 97   5 4 3 2 1

The Wick First Book Series is sponsored by the Stan and Tom Wick Poetry Program and
the Department of English at Kent State University.

Library of Congress Cataloging-in-Publication Data

Willey, Rosemary, 1959–
      Intended place : poems / by Rosemary Willey.
          p.   cm. — (Wick poetry first book series)
      ISBN 0-87338-581-0 (cloth : alk. paper). —ISBN 0-87338-584-5 (pbk. : alk. paper)
      I. Title.   II. Series.
      PS3573.I44725I58   1997   97-12240
      811'.54—dc21   CIP

British Library Cataloging-in-Publication data are available.

for Margaret

CONTENTS

ACKNOWLEDGMENTS

Some of these poems first appeared in the following magazines, sometimes in slightly different versions: "Return Flight," *Cimarron Review;* "Dreams in the Seventh Month," *Crazyhorse;* "Riverside Cemetery, December" and "Morning Parable," *Encore Magazine;* "Wishing the Neighbors Goodnight," *Green Mountains Review;* "The Fitting Room," *Indiana Review;* "Nightmares and Prayers of Rescue," *Kalliope: A Journal of Women's Art;* "All the Needs," *Poetry;* "As It Is," *Poetry Miscellany;* "The House We Pass Through," *Ploughshares.*

The following poems have dedications: "White Flowers," for Lissa Lutz (1959–1995); "Massage," for Robin Baugher; "Markham Street, Toronto," for John and Greg.

I'd like to acknowledge the help and encouragement of my excellent teachers at Vermont College. My thanks to William Matthews, Alane Rollings, and especially Maggie Anderson for their advice and support. I am grateful to Deirdre McAllister for providing a place for me to write. My most heartfelt thanks I give to Charles.

ALL THE NEEDS

All the little tumblers
near the green pitcher,
the nesting bowls,
the rattle of spoons.
All the mittens lost
behind the radiator,
the rush and return
for what's forgotten—
lunch bag, book, stark
on the kitchen counter.
All the faces too near
the screen, Ed Sullivan,
my father barking,
"Sit back, sit back."
All the blessings,
then the beds,
all the needs left
until morning.
How could there be any secrets?
The clay pinch pots,
the coils of snakes.
All the books with
Scotch-taped pages,
snubbed down crayons,
missing colors.
All the homemade
store-bought clutter,
all the seedlings in the yard.
The endless cycle
of our clothing,
mother folding on the couch.
All the longing
to be older, all
the borrowed,
broken, gone.
The closets,
rifled in anger.

When we were finished,
what was left?
All the diaries
read by flashlight,
the circle dimming,
batteries dead.
All the silhouettes
by nightlight,
the sound of footsteps,
then of sleep.

THE FITTING ROOM

She thinks of other women who have stood
undressed in this glare.
Surrounded in paleness, she's stunned
at the profile of her nose, her round head.
She hurries to be dressed again,
easing her arms through vintage satin.
The dress settles effortlessly, not tight
as she zips it to her middle back
and squares her round shoulders above
the boat neckline, and all those
other women vanish. The salesman
wants to have a look, so she steps
to the center of the cramped thrift shop.
He tugs and smoothes the skirt and hooks
the little eye, while she flushes,
and, suddenly, she's prettier.
Oh, buy it, he urges, because he knows
she will, her head spinning and her body
still and sculpted. *It was made for you.*
She's sure it belonged to someone completely unlike her,
someone with an armoire of gowns,
with beaded shoes and long black gloves.
He calls his partner to see the dress swirl
and they watch while she begins to falter.
Don't deny yourself this, they almost plead,
and it's not that she would disappoint them,
but it seems such a big decision: to become
this other woman, to let the face in the mirror
become her face. She tilts and sways,
looks again at the dress she wears flawlessly,
the dress she could wear in May,
the dress she could wear dancing.
Take your time, they tell her, watching
her slip behind the worn velvet drape.

AS IT IS

From across the room where you are sitting
I must look busy.
I am reading Hikmet.
I am seriously considering my own "Hymn to Life."
But I'm having trouble.
First of all, I cannot sit very long without
thinking about the roll on my stomach that
presses uncomfortably at the top of my pants.
I get up, walk back and forth
around the apartment until
you suggest I go out.

On the street people walk in clusters
and those who are alone seem at least accompanied
by their destinations.
If I were going somewhere, I'm sure it would show
on my face the same way: those quick glances
that case the street for its hard facts only.
But I'm reading house numbers.

If, like Hikmet, I were on the inside for years,
I'm sure I could arrive at the pure feeling
of a February afternoon and nothing to do
but walk the street where I live. I could
drench myself in the details
of this fattening life, discovering them
as if for the first time. I would be grateful.
                              As it is,
I'll write my hymn to say that most of my life
I've spent waiting—
for trains, for dinner, for a good night's sleep—

which is a captivity unlike prison
because it feels deserved.
                        As it is,
my hymn will say that days like this one
are forgiven. It does not need to be so
eloquent—this day, the hymn, my life.
677, 679, 13, 15, 17—House numbers begin
again after a gap I somehow missed.
The squirrels here are dusty and thin.
Street intermittently light as I wind my way back.

DREAMS IN THE
SEVENTH MONTH

I don't dream the murderous old lover dream
    anymore, nor the one where I'm driving cross-country
        with my dying grandparents in the back seat.

These nights my dreams pour in thick,
    intricate montage, and there's nothing to do
        but lie still while the stars form a glass

pitcher above my roof and sleep lifts the ceiling.
    I am waiting for a woman in a vinyl booth,
        or on a foreign train descending a mountain.

It's snowing, and I'm trying to save someone from ruin,
    I'm driving or running and somehow both in the dream
        and stepping back, struggling to remember

that boy's name, that town. Waking, I'll remember
    the scene and the struggle, lying tangled
        in the wisp of cool air from the partly open window,

bringing in the scent of something waiting for,
    not leaving: the way autumn suddenly
        smells like spring with its memories of backyards,

of you in your fine young body, turning,
    brushing a leaf from your hair. Nothing finishes,
        I can't distinguish what is real and what is dream.

I still see the numbered room where I slept
    on a cot beneath a blade of light, and early morning
        the damp walk below where I tried to write in chalk

but the words wouldn't take. In the blur of the pool,
    weightless and without my glasses, pregnant women
        dot the surface, floating silently, barely moving.

I must be dreaming, and this time I'm afraid
   of slipping on wet tile. I'm taking these cumbersome
      steps barefoot along the pool's edge.

It's a dream of caution, a dream of weight
   that lightly gives way, lapsing from final scene
      to scene, promising nothing but holding me like water.

Along this stretch of highway red-tails dot
the trees with their tucked shapes.
Serena knows where to spot them:
on billboards, telephone poles, beneath
the shadows of an overpass. She knows
the strategy of a solid perch, not too high,
on the edges of fields where they catch mice.
She brushes the auburn bangs from her eyes,
clutching the wheel of my old car she keeps
resurrecting. I decide to tell her
not to wear that baggy coat.
"There!" she cries, pointing
to a hawk that hangs like a harbinger.
"Red-tailed . . . *definitely,*" she tells me.
I remind her to turn at exit twelve.
I wish she would be more careful,
she's counting goddamn red-tails as if
they were the scattered bits of her defiance.
We see a tree with a dark spot in its branches.
The hawk pulls toward us like gravity—
square head, cleft shoulders, huge, prize-winning!
Serena brings the car to a dead halt
as my lap fills with pellets, bones,
feathers falling from the dashboard.

FOUR BLOCKS

Out the door and my head starts to drone:
What to wring from this dull week?
There's the usual November weather: bleak.
There's the usual sodden leaves: autumn's
litter at every curb and along the schoolyard
fence where a swarm of children's jackets blur.
A dryer vents across my path its vaporous
scented mist. The next block only my hard
shoes hitting the cement I know is cold. Maybe
I'm early and she's on the phone. I raise
a slow finger to the bell and the lock frees
with a long, jarring buzz and then I pace the lobby,
in my head a daring, spirited conversation
that always ends, *Good work, good session.*

WHERE IT COMES FROM

First I bring it to the table, feeling
gutsy enough to bid spades, but then I stop
to ask where it comes from: the slouched
shoulders, bad back? The stomach, or lower?
Because it isn't on the outside anymore,
it isn't spiritual. I want to give it color
when it's clearly black and white, but
I'm rushing and wouldn't the scent be more
than cigarettes or the stale breath left
on the receiver? When I think it's diminished,
it leaves me sleepless. Like water I poured
and forgot to drink, it distracts me in mid-
thought. A bare nail, a cut-short quarrel,
oblique as my father and turned to blue.

BELIEVABLE

That inescapable animal walks with me . . .
                                    Delmore Schwartz

The picture is complicated:
a vivid day at the Children's Zoo.
But look: some are upside down,
some have one shoe.

A polar bear strays and follows me
to my dinged-up station wagon,
me with my bomber jacket and cigarette,
Bono blaring on the radio station

and what's wrong with this picture?
The bear is believable, but now he's gone
and I'm meeting my friends
at the restaurant, the only woman

at the table, stockings and a little heel.
I love them all, but something's wrong.
Can you pick the friend I lose?
Gallant in an ivory tux, the young

waiter leads us out to a meadow
dotted with crumbling gravestones
and two white bears who circle
each other as they trade pedestals,

then bow when we clap. In bed
with my husband, the recurring
dream of a dancing bear at the mall.
I know it's wrong for something

fierce to be set loose in the aisle,
but it doesn't bother other shoppers.
We wake as the children jump on the bed
and I roll to find my daughter's

brought back the bear, small and stuffed.
I stare into the black bead eye.
What's wrong with this picture?
Nothing stricken, nothing strayed.

FROM THE MIDDLE

Mother tells us it's worse
when there's no further down to go,
when the milk is powdered,
the clothes from church.

We sleep to the tinny hum
of the fan lodged in the hall window,
voices rising from the porch.
It's summer and we go barefoot.
We steal coins from the jar.
We fight till one of us tastes blood.

From the middle, it all seems
ordinary, but then I hear
my oldest sister crying on the phone:
I can't stand it anymore. Get me the hell out of here.
There's a hot, late sun slanting
across the house and something's
burning on the stove, somebody swears.

Tonight the doors swell
with damp heat, the dog barks and barks.
Why won't our mattresses lift
like flying carpets and we spiral up,
the house small as a speck?

MORNING PARABLE

Acorns drop on her house
like stones thrown by boys.

Colors glint through the trees
but it's only light in the leaves.

She finds no stones, no boys.
In this dim hour her trouble

is plain: *How do I sleep
with all this racket?*

This worthless fruit?

NOT YOU

The one you don't leave.
The one you've bolstered
for so long there's pain
like a knee in your back.
The one whose skin across the sheets
is like something you knew once.
The one who saw you first.
The one who let this happen.

The one whose bareness
at the sink is like memory,
who raised you from the chair,
cupping your elbows until
you kissed. The one
who says *pick your poison.*
The one who took you from that town.

The one who rubs the pain.
The one who won't say it,
who just prefers it.
The one whose cruelty
is like memory, who says
you can't see the forest.
The one who asks *what do you want?*

The one who raised you up
from all your burdens,
who took you from that town.
The one you don't leave.
The one who says *you make a better door.*
You make a better door.

AGORAPHOBIC

It blinds her, the sunset splintering
the lake's surface, the singular thing
she can't escape. It could be the past.
It could be the body she will not love.
There's a stone in her sandal, a bee
spirals her midriff. She stops
on the narrow walk that leads to her door.
She's asking her house to let her go,
imagining no one is waiting
and this would be happening
whether she was woman or ghost.

She has trouble lately remembering names,
the confusion of left and right,
what year to pen in the small blank
on her check. In careful script
she lists the hopeful *courses à faire,*
checks her hair in the rearview
and drives herself to the market.
She lingers too long in the far aisle
where wet vegetables gleam, until
she hears *romaine, vidalia, plum tomato*
and begins to fill her cart.

Her voice guides her through this task,
wanting her to be better at this,
her reflection less pale. But she's
thick with errands and despair,
the faces of friends loved and out-lived,
the gradual diminishing of marriage,
past lovers surfacing in dreams.
The steady reminders of the life
she doesn't live, in the harsh market,
surrounded in primary colors and the jars
marked with identical, doll-like faces.

Ghost or woman, she's heading home
with the captive brown bags
jostling in the back seat. She finds
she's turning toward the lake,
so bright she shields her eyes.
She can't turn from the shimmering light.
She can't shake whatever it is
that draws her under this open sky,
the water gleaming its sheet of hammered silver
across what she knows is blue,
underneath, what she knows is endless.

WHITE FLOWERS

Today my friend has the strength to walk.
She wants burgers and shakes at a picnic table
in Soldier's Field, Rochester, Minnesota.

We're old friends, two girls in the park,
in the high school photograph, in the blue Chevette
we drove down to the dunes that lined

the beaches of our town. We are the girls who
burned a pentagram in the field behind
the Mussleman's plant, pricked our fingers

and chanted from the stolen library book.
Girls mixing blood, swapping nicknames, slamming
the front doors of our plain, inescapable houses.

She blames her husband for the headaches,
how nights he visualizes over video games,
PacMen eating tumors in battles he wins

for her. For her it's white flowers imagined
in each dose of radiation. She whispers it,
flicking her fingers open, *white flowers,*

and I see them too, though she doesn't say what kind.
She's wringing whatever joy she can from this
dismal Oz, her four block radius from the clinic,

the room she's rented in a cheap motel.
But I am not that girl anymore. I don't use
that old nickname. She insists on nothing

but who we were, takes the strained, deliberate
steps to lead us back. What's happening now
we leave unnamed. On the morning before I go

she sends me down for free donuts and I face
the other tenants who linger in the lobby
and I don't want to leave her here.

Near the window where she sleeps I tape
a silk bouquet. We take pictures
at the car and she's left her hat in the room.

The motel clerk snaps the picture:
two girls shoulder to shoulder, squinting
in the sun against the chipped stucco facade.

THE BOY IN THE PARK

I was told not to touch him, not to let him
touch me, the head teacher explained how
he escaped into touch, the body's warmth,

slipping back through his six short years
to infancy, his limbs becoming slack.
But because Brian was happy he seemed less

lost than the other children. At a desk
behind a tall screen he'd crawl onto my lap
and rock with a deliberate rhythm.

I'd let my arms wrap around his curled back
and finish the song fragments he murmured
while he blinked up at me, surprised.

He could do the math, scrawling rote numbers
without a pause. I turned in the pages,
walked home wistful with the feeling of

Brian in my arms, like something you could
blow away or break. Nothing was so simple then
as the pang to love a strange child,

though today I flinch from the boy scuffing
in the park toward his mother, cradling his hands
like downed birds, just the way Brian did

before I'd press a pencil into his thin palm
and close the span of fingers. The truth is
I held him only once, afraid of getting caught,

of letting the others see my inability
to follow rules. I wanted him to remember me,
our afternoons, my name, though he could

not say it. That summer I wanted to say
goodbye but he broke from me, flailing his hands
and letting go a string of sounds above the park.

NIGHTMARES AND
PRAYERS OF RESCUE

In this bad dream sheets drift thick with snow
and I lie motionless in the woods, my figure
muted under shadows of gray, knowing
you might never find me, obscured
and barely breathing. If I were left for dead,
don't bother why or how, just promise
it will be you who kneels to brush a red
glove across my back, marring the blank canvas
I'm lost in. I've heard tales of lovers who
find each other, even when war-torn or
kidnapped. I pray this sense is in you too:
to track me down before I disappear, before,
catching my breath beneath the white linen,
I wake with my head full of brutal men.

WHAT WAS BRILLIANCE

Half-awake on the sofa, the crane's
whine escalating from down the block,
I sit up and she's naked in the kitchenette,
one pointed elbow tipping a steaming kettle.
She laughs at my modesty as I struggle

into jeans, regretting her offer,
her insistence, that I stay another night.
She hopes I like my coffee strong.
On the street I want to forget her body
and the way she looked at mine—

perhaps the body she'd had, childless and younger.
Forget the slang and innuendo of her
drunk hours, the times her look
could be mistaken for loathing,
hating me for the mistakes I hadn't made.

I've made them now. That day, the west side
was treacherous with construction,
the unearthed blocks poorly fenced
where I walked the makeshift detours
painted in fluorescent arrows,

in my pocket the clipped address—
Roommate Wanted—I tossed into the street.
Her letters brought me there: *not that
New York was right for me,* she wrote,
but I was right for it, peddling

a dream she'd always had: to shed
the midwestern girl she was, the girl
I met in school. I didn't know
it was as simple as her need to keep
some piece of a past that saved her:

me at nineteen, my reverence, struck
by what I thought was brilliance.
I didn't know the comfort we find
in not belonging, the way we orphan
ourselves from whatever hurt us.

But I knew that if I stayed another night
she'd drink and talk of her failed marriage,
the son she left, her dead father
whose mention muted her voice.
And I'd think *you were beautiful,*

watching her face slacken from across
the table until I'd help her to bed.
I'd lie awake beneath the weight
of my loyalty slipping, my conversion, my wish
to be rid of her so clear I can almost

join myself in flight, hailing a taxi
before dawn, past the billboard's
promise of a bold high-rise to be,
like the one I find years later, here
and here, and nothing of her anywhere.

GOOD FORTUNE

Last night the classroom dream:
the squared desks spread with maps
and mine unreadable, impossible
to decipher. And yet today
I'm driving in this dense fog
thinking how no one in my family
has seen Vermont in any season,
how in this small way I'm amazing.
I'm meeting a friend who's marrying
the man she's loved for three years.
It's late summer and I'm reviewing
the little film loop of my life,
how strange to be strapped
in this steel-blue rental car
with my flat San Pellegrino,
on the radio Strauss's *Four Last Songs*.
I'm reminding myself how bad it's been,
the relative good fortune of now.
Certainly you already know this.
I'm cautious but driving fast
enough to feel the curves' suction,
the pretty, tireless landscape
seeping from its blanket of gauze.
Tonight I'll dine with my beautiful friend
and she'll break my heart with her happiness.
This I'm certain you already know.

RIVERSIDE CEMETERY, DECEMBER

He thought of how he must look
from the first houses, the passing cars,
trudging uphill against the wind with her

close behind in a scarlet coat,
stalking the graveyard in such stark weather,
pausing at these plain graves.

He brushed snow from the flat headstones—
eight of them, the last his grandmother's—
and shouted the lineage from grave to grave

for her to hear through a hat and scarf.
She listened carefully until it seemed
she too was conscious of the sight of them.

Why had he shown her any of this?
If his grandmother had lived in another time
there would be no grave, he assured himself.

She would have had her ashes set free
across the meadows behind her house
where he played as a boy. She would be

carried on the stream that split the land,
and under the bridge he built as a young man.
How little there is to show here:

grandmother in what seems to be her proper place,
amid a frozen landscape set with stones,
the sky and snow without distinction.

POTTER'S TAVERN

Whenever we drive past this spot
Charlie mentions it: the time when a woman
stepped in front of our car.
I remember her in close-up,
unbelievable since I only saw her
for a frantic, swerving moment
from the passenger side,
slowing just enough to make
the feeling, the image, stick.
In this bare landscape her face
hid nothing. Scared but fierce,
she stood frozen for a split
second, staring crazed at me.
A man just yards from her,
his face flushed, hands fisted,
screamed furiously but waited
until we passed
to yank her off the road.
Drunk, I said. *Drunk and fighting.*
Charlie muttered *stupid bitch*
and I felt a cold hardening
in the air, winter in the dry
grasses, these pale fields.
How passively the seasons cover this spot
just past Potter's Tavern,
always colorless as snow.
How clearly I can see her eyes,
the wish there, still piercing
the comfort of my ride home.
We would have hit her,
if not for the oncoming car which
cleared the lane so Charlie could pass.
Hit square into her messy life.

That would have sucked, he says now,
Potter's fading in the stretch behind us.
I know he means more than the simple
matter of police and ambulances
and people we wouldn't want to meet.
I know how little it takes
to enter one disastrous life,
the tragedies we play no part in ending.

THE STAIN

My brothers never saw the girl
who spied on us through the fence where we played
while the sky dimmed and we grew tired and thirsty
before mother called us in. I'd linger
to be last then looked back to see her
peering at me from between the slats.
Once I heard crying and I went out alone to face her.
She'd snagged her hand on a nail in the fence
and held it to me while I stopped the blood.
I hated her soft sobs, her flattened brown bangs.
Go home, I whispered, as heat lightning bristled
and a warm rain broke in splats along our arms.
Go before they see you. Mother didn't ask
about the small stain at my shirt hem. It purpled
and grayed and I knew she'd probably never ask.
They said I was a liar when you didn't come back.
But you were as real as any loss I could trace
in those shortening days,
faded mouth, pale oxbrow, pitiful girl.

LATE WITH GRANDMOTHER

She's back in Pittsburgh,
While from the sink I hand her
Each shining white plate.

She says I'm a small
Part of a marvelous world,
Lucky and young.

Now comes the one boy
She loved, though she did nothing.
Now comes the moon.

TWO SISTERS

It would be simplest to say
One hates me
Because I didn't choose
Her to love,
But that would be untrue.

I am most like the one I love:
The sister who wakes me.
Our hair is the same.
Our language the same.
When we walk she says
"See the finch dive from tree to tree?"
"The bird is a fish," I say.

The sister who hates me
Comes late, pounding
Her fist on my door.
When I open the door
She calls me "Fool."

I claim my bad sister.
I claim her because
She sends me such perfect grief:
Her cold heart
In a paper box.
Who would do this if not her?
"Hate me," I say.
We all live with our own trouble.

My good sister dances
With hands like blossoms,
Arms slender as stems.
My bad sister spins
And spatters me
With green tears.

MY UNDOING

for my daughter

I lie to her about the times
I cry and cool my face
on the shower tile.
I lie about the words I use
that don't exist.
There will be much to undo
as she is my undoing,
my innumerable hours, water
poured between two cups.

There's a man pumping gas,
the round turquoise buckle
on his belt circling our car.
There are whirlpools of leaves
spinning in the mall courtyard,
wind billowing her dress
as I sweep her up in the rain.
The sky above the parking lot
gray and radiant.
I'm so tired, I say,

but whatever she loves she wants
again, as I want the same plea
and curve of her damp face.
Nothing happens more than once,
I explain and think again before bed,
her body, flushed from the bath,
across the bed like the brown girl
in *Spirit of the Dead Watching.*
Glazed, near sleep, she slips
from the numinous world
she gives and does not know.

THE HOUSE WE PASS THROUGH

It is just a family. I am just a girl
posing at the mirror in a flowered
cotton shift, combing back my short hair,
deciding whether I'm beautiful. I know
the creak in the floor by heart and the hiss
of the door behind me, drawing itself shut.
When I cross the room, my brothers and sisters
don't care, their faces turn to the tv set.
From under the basement stairwell I see
my mother lifting laundry from the dryer,
my oldest brother behind her, white as a sheet.
The *slosh, slosh* of the washer muffles my mother's
words. *Buck up, Buck up,* I hear her warning.
The next of us is about to be born.

BEFORE WE MOVE

To all the places I've left in my life
I've already added this one, though
because of her there's something more:

what's added when you take a child
from the only home she's ever known,
the subtle work of how best

not to disturb her sleep.
Thus the conspiracy begins, with
all the delicacies of any major task,

whispered plans and night packing,
the decisions of what to conceal under
the thinning surface of our days.

Let me tell you what I promise:
this apartment will become a house,
this city, a smaller town.

She asks about what will no longer be
her garden and the stash of pebbles
and sticks she keeps along the wall.

I see a yard hung with red ball feeders,
hummingbirds disappearing
in a summer of late copper lilies—

a promised future she does not see,
brimming with the things she has not thought
to wish for. Before we move I say

goodbye to the dutiful trees
that marked my seasons for six years,
with their wine-colored buds, the sway

of green, so particular in its passing.
Change comes. But she conceals
nothing in what she knows, and watches

the shelves mysteriously bare themselves
by morning, while her notion of permanence
begins its own swift departure.

BUILDING CHARACTER

This is as good as it gets:
reminiscing with old friends after dinner
and still sitting at the cluttered table.
Of course I am stronger, though not quite
hardened yet. Not disappointed,
too soon for that. My friend,
when she was dying, never acted like
she knew it, as if it were my job
to know and hers simply to do. So
I tacked her photograph to the wall
where I still write and imagined life
without her, rehearsed the healing
conversations and the recollections
of our bedside visits that went so well,
like the one where she took me in her arms
as if I were finally getting it right.
This is how it feels to feel better,
I'm telling my surviving friends,
what it means to be older, the past
building its scaffolding up my spine.
I'm telling them it's worth it,
I'm toasting to just how much,
though whomever I call tonight—
my guests all gone—it won't be her,
the one who knew what I stood to lose.

RETURN FLIGHT

The young woman across the aisle
has slipped off her blouse, camisoled
in the hot plate, a strand of onyx

beads draped against her skin.
It's hard to glimpse her beyond
my husband's paper, showing so much

freckled skin, her hair a rare
autumnal rust, narrowing her face
and reaching in waves to her elbows.

She keeps brushing it from her bare
shoulders, lifting it in damp handfuls
from her neck, and I wonder if

I've ever touched hair that color.
I don't know what it's like
to leave somebody, forget the string

of sorrows learned to live with
and part. It's soothing
to stare down at life from this distance,

to see how perfectly it all fits—
a patchwork, a puzzle, finished as if
each town, each street and house

had found its intended place.
The woman is in her blouse now,
eating fragrant orange sections

she's wrapped in a napkin, wiping
her fingers on her lap. Later,
she tilts back into a deep sleep,

her jaw dropped, lips parted
like the drowned girl
in Millais's *Ophelia*. She drifts

while we descend, my husband
offering me his paper as I turn
to see my view obscured by clouds.

ALL IS QUIET

Across the hall, 3B, they are grieving
for their lost child. I knock to find
their kitchen littered with pastel envelopes,
unswept petals. And yesterday, 2D,
dying of AIDS, hid his scabbed chest
when I startled him on the roof deck,
so I looked out across the rooftops
and in the silence I realized no one
in 2C was begging for mercy or forgiveness.
All is quiet, except for me, 3A, shuttling
the halls with warm soup and ice, the one
who brings the paper, the one who brings word.
Seen grimly through the crack of the door,
I'm also the one who wants to forget them,
the one who stands there muttering.
But it's me they see wherever they look,
it is my words when they speak.
My fingers dial relatives, nurse the sores,
my heart divides again and again.
Me, 3A, cupping my hand to the flame,
5B, twisting the fuse with my finger and thumb,
2D, potting marigolds in the window box.
I am grieving a child who will not come
to the table again, I am closing a book and
turning to kiss you, I am weeping outside the door.

RESOLUTE

In spite of the wind we pause to watch
a noisy flock of crows as they set down
on yet another thin snow on this road.
My young daughter squeezes my hand.
All March a dull storm that won't pass, a sun
too weak to break through, and the knowledge
I kept shapeless on the inside
finds this moment to be visceral and clear.
Whatever I've done, I meant no harm.
I'll protect my house though all the myths
have left it now. She runs and pulls me,
our coats flutter in the sudden gust that cuts
between us, and I find I couldn't be
more hers—this girl, nearly mythic, mine.

MASSAGE

It's the unfinished
Bound Slaves in the corridor
that the guide finds particularly important,
but a sudden flock

of blazered schoolboys
swipes your interest into the cool
dome where David towers in his one and only pose.
They snicker and flinch

beneath him, exotic
dark-eyed boys you have seen
all over this city, faces foreshadowing the men
they will become.

Perhaps
it's the stone color
of the walls that conjures this scene from the past,
your body

draped in sheets
as the masseuse warms your
oiled back and you feel you're falling, tangled—
amber and brown

of the riverfront,
twelve years ago, the last time
he disappeared beneath the black umbrella,
the first time

you felt the limits
of your heart. In a low voice
she names the trouble: *Too much sitting*
at your desk,

too many hurried
errands, too wound up to sleep
last night, too much strain, too much alone.
The secrets

of a bad week
packed between your shoulders.
And you hear another voice, you see the men
emerging as

the guide speaks:
Here is the body, subtracted
from stone. What is finished is perfect, while
the rest, seized

in marble, waits.
You hurry from the Galleria,
the Arno pocked by rain. You balance yourself
in the rippled glass

at the pensione
window, before you heave
the shutters out to the noisy street, the sky
tarnished again.

NIGHTFALL, NEW YORK

You left him sauntering up Broadway
  in a tan peacoat, wrapped
    in his own ponderous evaporation,

easier without the freight
  of a long-drawn farewell.
    The gust from the cab window

drowns the Jamaican driver's lilt
  as you joined the headlights beading
    the Bridge toward Brooklyn,

and it felt like being pulled,
  knowing this time was for good,
    the skyline sagging in the rearview.

Maybe you were not so drunk, just
  afraid to let sadness loosen
    into such an empty space—

nineteen boxes plus assorted furniture,
  ready to roll, with or without you.
    You could trace graphpaper rooms

where a foot equals an inch,
  and practice with cut-out shapes
    how your things would fit this new place,

study the strategies of the rooms
  with southern exposure, and for once,
    closets. But there is no shape

to cut for whatever's left behind
  and you couldn't plan how your dreams
    would brim with the past, holding

the thin rectangle of bed between
　　your fingers, a dark blue luster
　　　spreading on the harbor

where you're standing on the edge
　　of Brooklyn, saying goodbye to him
　　　as if to an uncle you hardly know.

LOST MUG

I summon back the morning before it's gone,
in search of my coffee cup, a cobalt blue,
poured and placed where I don't remember.

Meticulous and full of purpose, I find
myself orbiting the apartment while
a cool draft skims my ankles

and pipes clang with steam. I'm doubling,
passing the mirror like a ghost of myself.
I was here, then there, when the phone rang:

the neighbor's news of our flooded basement.
But what help would I be without my coffee?
The rooms, a flowchart of my habits, veer

wherever that blue taunts, until a suspicion
unfurls: the thought of someone else
circling with me a few paces ahead or behind,

a parallel person who knows when
to fill whatever space I've emptied,
eats when I sleep and bathes when I eat,

shrinks the soap and lets the cat in the hall.
And it does not unsettle me. I would leave
if I could, find a house to the north

where the lake view drenches the empty rooms.
A house with a dark, paneled library,
a kitchen hung with copper pots,

guestrooms untouched and readied
from which I'd choose the largest bed,
as if I knew the lake would rise and flood

the house and this bed would float me back
to my own, the cold mug returned to my hand
and I to a morning I can't retrieve.

MARKHAM STREET, TORONTO

So uninspired, the brick row house
in the center of the block,
but the realtor kept bringing you back,
until you imagined your furniture
invisibly placed here and there,
the rooms another color, until—
pausing on the stairs—you could almost hear
your lover asking for water, for you
not to be long. Word came
that you bought the house. Now
you walk to work past these slab gardens
as the shaggy peonies begin to droop,
the ice-blue plaster draping
beneath Mary's turned-out palms.
You're not certain how to greet
the old neighbor at his gate,
that cigarette he never seems to finish,
or if the work's already done
and he knows all there is to know,
nodding as you frisk for your keys.
And what is there to know?
How difficult for you and he to buy
this place, how difficult to call it home—
not fearlessly enough to believe it,
still too afraid not to try. Everything's
larger than it ought to be, but
leaving room enough to wonder
if this will be the last place,
these walls the last surfaces of light.
The first night of my visit
I thumbed a book from your shelf
on "visualizing," where one imagines

good t-cells gathered like a choir
to heal the bad. I tried to journey
down inside my chest to the lungs and heart,
the spidery network of veins, but
it was hollow space, the black
on black of my body against the bed
as, blindly, I traveled into sleep.
When I awoke I saw the rooftops
sloping out beyond the alley, the same
moss-green asphalt as out my girlhood
bedroom window. I could still see
the girl I was sunning herself
in the wavy trapped heat, an old towel
spread on the grainy roof under
a wedge of sky I claimed as my own.
Today my friends will take me walking
and I'll lock eyes with the young
Portugese men loitering on the corner.
The sun streaming all afternoon
will saturate the multiple shades of brick,
the huge zucchini someone has grown
in a chain-link cage. Today we'll
feel as though we're not our bodies,
we're more than what we cherish
and cannot keep. This house—
transformed now with a little paint,
adorned with your collection of
ceramic fish—on Markham Street
where, if I close my eyes, I'll picture you.

WISHING THE
NEIGHBORS GOODNIGHT

Across the alley the old woman undresses
for bed, her shutters slightly open,
the light behind her dim. It is discreet,
the way nudity can gently insist
we are human. Already
we have much in common: the way
she folds her pants over a chair,
returns her blouse to its empty hanger
and loosens a nightgown around her.
Her husband plays solitaire at the window
where he always sits, his hands,
like a pianist's, rising and falling.
Her arms rise to tie a net for her hair.
All this takes a long time.
From my dark kitchen, well past the dishes,
I tally the small gestures
in my most precious days, most precious nights.
Black king, red queen, aces in a row.
She moves through the frame
twice before the light goes out.

FLY AWAY HOME

I needed to break my four o'clock habits,
and it seemed the spike tree could be made to look
like Christmas. With my thumb against a blade,
I curled paper ribbon, while in Armenia
there was an earthquake. The television
camera pans a crumbled street: *rubble*.
Survivors huddle closely together, their faces

downcast in grief. With both arms a woman circles
the air around her, her hands clasp over her heart,
then—as if on their own—they rise again,
circling air and dust, perhaps her vanished home.
The bodies of children are found like lost dolls,
ruined and dirty. Gorbachev leaves New York early,
waving grimly from the plane, his wife in black,

and our own president sends a message:
"I'm sure all Americans would extend a warm hand
to those families in need." The search
for bodies will last weeks. Yesterday
I cried for no reason. It seemed the thing to do,
like tonight, suddenly spirited, I decorate
a gangly tree, as if I'd won my own argument,

and such celebration was in order. But I don't
have music for this moment, except what the past
has left: the sound of crisp tissue, of china and silver,
the cluttering voices of relatives among
my own family. I don't have angels with trumpets,
tin birds, and shiny glass balls that reflect
my huge grin in gold tree light. In these memories

I am always the child—my hands unwrapping
a book of rhymes, my nose touching its smell—
but somehow the child is not me. Now I want
to see myself in this warm scene: this
Woman with Eggnog and Slippers, but when
I get the bad news I recall my bewildered face
last week in the thick airplane window—

a layover in Detroit—as congratulations were
announced and one by one an Armenian wedding party
paraded down the aisle to the back of the plane,
their arms balancing flowers and gifts and
countless beautiful children. The bride
in a long ermine coat was followed by several
bearded men, the groom indistinguishable among

the flushed faces. The steward explained how
in New York they would join families,
how the celebration would last for days.
The cabin dimmed and filled with the smell
of wine and I decided my own life
was unchangeable. Tonight, when I am already
sick of memory, I hear of this country again,

recalling how quickly I fled from the airport,
the faint cheers of reunion at my back. Tonight
the television updates endlessly the story,
raising the death toll, the bodies pulled from
crushed homes until they become familiar.
I shut it off as the screen fills with
the flying silhouettes of geese and remember

a whole page of colored sky, diving white birds,
their long necks heading them in all directions:
Ladybird, Ladybird, fly away home,
Your house is on fire, your children all gone.
I stand at the mirror and circle my arms
like the grieving woman. Now I understand
her gesture, the eruption, its center.

Imagine pain as if the heart were breaking,
the lungs too full, falling too empty. Imagine
ribs gripping something so powerful the body
could not contain it, had to let it go, so
the hands fly up as if to say: *This circle is my life,*
what's left at this moment, what's made it this far,
without crumbling, without vanishing.